SAVING EARTH'S BIOMES

RESTORING THE GREAT BARRIER REEF

by Rachel Hamby

FOCUS
READERS®
NAVIGATOR

WWW.FOCUSREADERS.COM

Focus Readers is distributed by North Star Editions:
sales@northstareditions.com | 888-417-0195

Produced for Focus Readers by Red Line Editorial.

Content Consultant: Jesse Zaneveld, Assistant Professor of Biological Sciences, University of Washington, Bothell

Photographs ©: Aaron Bull/iStockphoto, cover, 1; Norbert Probst/imageBROKER/Alamy, 4–5; Red Line Editorial, 7, 15; Darkydoors/Shutterstock Images, 9; atese/iStockphoto, 10–11; Damsea/Shutterstock Images, 13; tae208/iStockphoto, 17; Beachy Photography/ Shutterstock Images, 18–19; Caleb Jones/AP Images, 21; D. Parer & E. Parer-Cook/Minden Pictures/Newscom, 23; Norman Kuring/Ocean Color Web/Aqua MODIS/NASA, 24–25; Alexandros Michailidis/Shutterstock Images, 27; Huw Thomas/iStockphoto, 29

Library of Congress Cataloging-in-Publication Data
Names: Hamby, Rachel, 1970- author.
Title: Restoring the Great Barrier Reef / by Rachel Hamby.
Description: Lake Elmo, MN : Focus Readers, [2020] | Series: Saving earth's biomes | Includes index. | Audience: Grades 4-6
Identifiers: LCCN 2019034468 (print) | LCCN 2019034469 (ebook) | ISBN 9781644930694 (hardcover) | ISBN 9781644931486 (paperback) | ISBN 9781644933060 (pdf) | ISBN 9781644932278 (ebook)
Subjects: LCSH: Great Barrier Reef (Qld.)--Juvenile literature. | Coral reef restoration--Australia--Great Barrier Reef (Qld.)--Juvenile literature.
Classification: LCC QH541.5.C7 H355 2020 (print) | LCC QH541.5.C7 (ebook) | DDC 333.95/5315309943--dc23
LC record available at https://lccn.loc.gov/2019034468
LC ebook record available at https://lccn.loc.gov/2019034469

Printed in the United States of America
Mankato, MN
012020

ABOUT THE AUTHOR

Rachel Hamby writes poetry, short fiction, and nonfiction for kids. She was born on the very first Earth Day in 1970. She enjoys writing books about the environment and hopes to inspire young scientists to ask questions and find answers.

TABLE OF CONTENTS

CHAPTER 1

A DYING REEF

The Great Barrier Reef is a colorful **ecosystem**. More than 400 types of coral build this living reef. Corals are animals. They also create homes for other forms of life. From snails to whales, many **species** depend on this natural wonder.

The Great Barrier Reef is the largest coral reef system on the entire planet.

Coral reefs support approximately 25 percent of all marine life.

5

This system includes coral reefs and islands. The reef is found off Australia's east coast. It stretches approximately 1,600 miles (2,500 km). Its size allows it to support many environments. For example, dugongs feed in seagrass beds. Green sea turtles lay eggs on island beaches. Saltwater crocodiles live in mangrove marshes.

The Great Barrier Reef supports humans as well. Many different groups of people have lived in the area for countless generations. They have lived there since long before Europeans colonized the land. Many have depended on the reef for a long time, too.

People continue to depend on the reef's fish for food. And tourists visit the reef from around the world. These visitors help bring money to Australia.

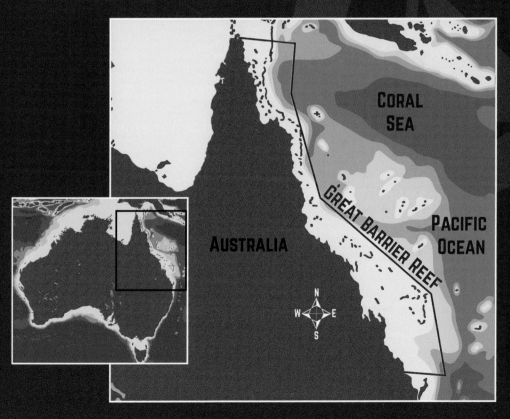

GREAT BARRIER REEF

CORAL SEA

GREAT BARRIER REEF

PACIFIC OCEAN

AUSTRALIA

Scientists use the reef as well. They make medicines from plants and animals there. However, the reef is in danger. **Climate change** is warming the oceans. Carbon dioxide is changing the water's makeup.

CORALS ARE ALIVE

Coral is made up of many polyps. Polyps grow together in **coral colonies**. They attach themselves to the ocean floor. Then these colonies build their own skeletons. The skeletons are white. But colorful microbes live inside the skeletons. These microbes get energy from the sun. They share this energy with corals. When a coral colony dies, its skeleton remains. Then it becomes part of the reef. New colonies attach to the reef. The Great Barrier Reef grew this way. The process took thousands of years.

Fish swim among dead coral in the Great Barrier Reef.

Pollution from farms and cities is harming the reef. As a result, corals are dying. Plants and animals are losing homes. People are losing an important resource.

Given time and the right conditions, corals can recover. They can rebuild damaged reefs. But this process can take years. With all the threats it faces, the Great Barrier Reef could be destroyed.

CHAPTER 2

THREATS TO THE REEF

The Great Barrier Reef faces a variety of threats. For example, people fish too much in some parts of the reef. Overfishing hurts the reef's **biodiversity**. When this happens, the reef becomes less able to survive other dangers.

Another problem is **runoff** from farms. Farmers use chemicals to grow crops.

The Great Barrier Reef is home to more than 1,500 species of fish, including clown fish.

Rain carries these chemicals to bodies of water, such as rivers. Then those bodies of water carry the waste into the ocean.

However, climate change is an even greater danger to the Great Barrier Reef. This crisis is making the reef waters warmer. Corals can only live in certain

GREENHOUSE GASES

Many power plants burn fuel to create energy. When fuel is burned, greenhouse gases enter the air. Carbon dioxide is one of these gases. Greenhouse gases trap heat. These gases are good in the right amounts. They help keep the planet warm. But current levels of greenhouse gases are too high. This increase is causing climate change.

The skeleton of a coral is visible after bleaching.

temperatures. When the water gets too hot, corals get rid of their microbes. Then coral skeletons become visible. They look white. This process is known as coral bleaching. When corals bleach too often, they run out of energy. Then they die. When many corals die quickly, plants and animals lose their homes.

The same greenhouse gases that cause climate change can also harm the reef in other ways. The level of carbon dioxide in the air is rising. And the oceans absorb that gas from the air. As a result, the oceans are taking in much more carbon dioxide. This change makes ocean water more **acidic**. Acidic water has fewer **nutrients**. Without those nutrients, corals cannot build strong skeletons. Weak corals break more easily during storms.

At the same time, climate change is also causing more extreme weather. Strong storms are hitting the Great Barrier Reef more often. These storms damage corals. They bring more runoff into the reef, too. As climate change gets worse, these problems will get worse as well. If trends continue, the reef may not have enough time to heal.

SEA TEMPERATURES IN THE GREAT BARRIER REEF

This graph shows how the reef's annual temperature compares to the ocean's average temperature.

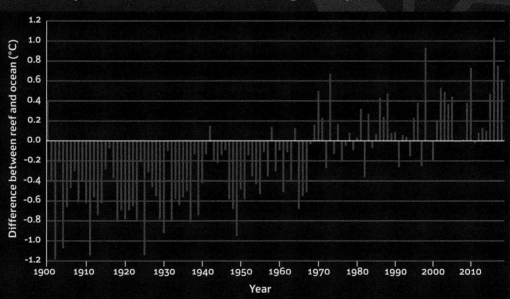

CROWN-OF-THORNS SEA STAR

Many crown-of-thorns sea stars live in the Great Barrier Reef. These sea stars have long spines. The spines are filled with poison. Some of these sea stars are purple. Others are red or green.

Crown-of-thorns sea stars eat corals. They often eat fast-growing corals. With fewer of those corals, slow-growing corals have space to grow. In this way, the sea stars tend to help the reef. A larger variety of corals makes the reef stronger.

However, sometimes a reef has an outbreak of these sea stars. An outbreak is when an area has more of something than usual. During outbreaks, the sea stars eat a lot of corals. The sea stars often eat corals faster than the corals can grow. When that happens, the reef weakens.

Crown-of-thorns sea stars can have more than 20 arms and hundreds of poisonous spines.

In the Great Barrier Reef, these outbreaks are happening more often. Increased runoff may be one cause. These sea stars are a natural part of the reef. But when the reef is weakened by runoff, the sea stars can be a problem for the reef's health.

CHAPTER 3

RESTORING THE REEF

The United Nations (UN) recognized the value of the Great Barrier Reef in 1981. The UN made the reef a World Heritage Area. This decision said that the reef needed to be cared for. The Australian government has taken some steps to help the reef. For example, it has declared some areas off-limits for fishing.

As of 2019, the Great Barrier Reef was one of only 213 natural World Heritage Areas on Earth.

In addition, some farmers are working to prevent runoff. They are trying to use fewer chemicals. Farmers are also planting trees in specific areas. These trees help stop chemicals from getting into the water.

Scientists and farmers are also working together. Scientists are learning how runoff works. They are learning how certain farms may harm parts of the reef. Then they share what they have learned with farmers. Those farmers can make changes.

Scientists are trying to restore the Great Barrier Reef in other ways. For instance, some are growing corals in labs.

In a lab, baby corals can grow much faster than they could in nature.

Then they attach the baby corals to weak reefs. The baby corals help the whole area heal.

Other scientists are helping important areas of the reef. Raine Island is one of these areas. Many green sea turtles travel to Raine Island in order to lay their eggs.

However, tides are flooding the island more often. Turtle eggs cannot survive underwater. In response, scientists are restoring the beaches. These efforts are helping save the turtles.

Unfortunately, none of these actions slow climate change. This crisis is one

TRADITIONAL OWNERS

The Wuthathi and Kemer Kemer Meriam nations are Traditional Owners of Raine Island. People from these nations are helping the animals on the island. For example, Peter Wallis and Jimmy Passi led teams to put up fences on the island. These fences stopped many turtles from falling off cliffs. Between 2017 and 2018, these efforts helped save 251 turtles.

Every year, up to 15,000 green sea turtles come to Raine Island to lay eggs.

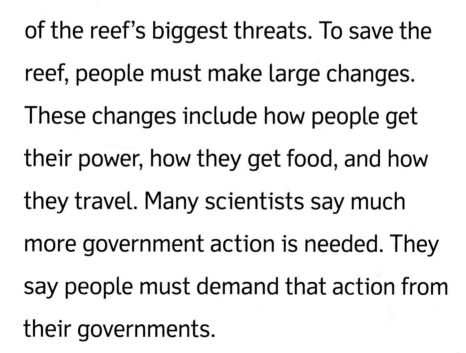

of the reef's biggest threats. To save the reef, people must make large changes. These changes include how people get their power, how they get food, and how they travel. Many scientists say much more government action is needed. They say people must demand that action from their governments.

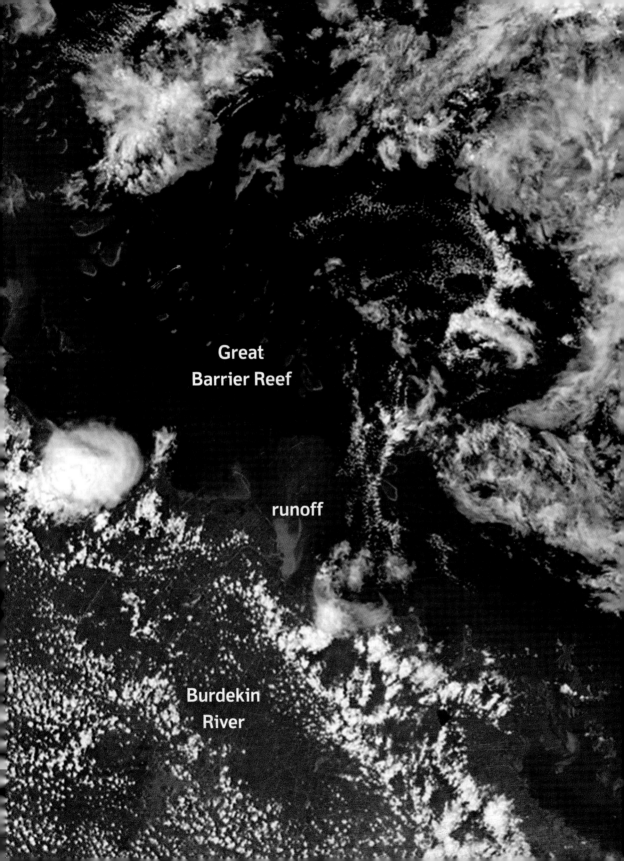

CHAPTER 4

LOOKING AHEAD

The Great Barrier Reef still faces many threats. Much more needs to be done. For example, farm runoff remains a danger to the reef. New laws require farmers to reduce their use of chemicals. But the Australian government has not been making sure that farmers follow these laws.

A picture from space shows farm runoff entering the Great Barrier Reef.

Climate change is already harming the Great Barrier Reef. In 2016 and 2017, mass bleaching hit the reef. Half of the reef's corals died. Looking ahead, climate change will become an even larger danger to the reef.

Massive action is needed to limit climate change. And in 2016, most of the world's countries signed the Paris Agreement. These countries agreed to address climate change. Many countries made changes. But in 2017, the United States said it would no longer be part of the agreement. And as of 2019, few countries were meeting the goals they had set.

In 2018, 15-year-old Greta Thunberg became a leading activist in the movement against climate change.

People have the ability to help address this problem. For example, countries can produce far fewer greenhouse gases. Certain sources of energy do not release those gases. These sources include wind and solar power. Using more of these sources is one of many needed changes.

Action needs to happen quickly. However, governments may not take these actions unless many people demand them.

Scientists are studying how to help the Great Barrier Reef survive climate change. For example, some corals can live in warm waters better than others. Scientists could grow more of these corals. Then the whole reef could become stronger. However, the Great Barrier Reef is huge. And planting new corals costs a lot of money.

Some scientists are also trying to guard the reef's plants and animals. They are creating climate change refuges. A refuge is a safe place. As reef waters

In 2019, scientists said that only the most extreme and quickest actions could help save the Great Barrier Reef.

warm, many species will lose their homes. But some of those species may find new homes in refuges.

The Great Barrier Reef faces more threats than ever before. But scientists continue to study ways to restore it. And people will keep working to help the Great Barrier Reef survive.

FOCUS ON
RESTORING THE GREAT BARRIER REEF

Write your answers on a separate piece of paper.

1. Write a paragraph that describes how climate change is harmful to the Great Barrier Reef.

2. Do you think current efforts to restore the Great Barrier Reef are enough? Why or why not?

3. What is one problem facing the Great Barrier Reef?

    A. too little fishing

    B. too much farm runoff

    C. too few crown-of-thorns sea stars

4. Why might climate change be getting worse?

    A. The ocean is not absorbing enough carbon dioxide.

    B. Warm water is heating the planet.

    C. Countries keep producing greenhouse gases.

Answer key on page 32.

GLOSSARY

acidic
A chemical property that makes some things taste sour.

biodiversity
The number of different species that live in an area.

climate change
A human-caused global crisis involving long-term changes in Earth's temperature and weather patterns.

coral colonies
Groups of hundreds or thousands of identical coral polyps that grow together.

ecosystem
A community of living things and how they interact with their surrounding environment.

nutrients
Substances that humans, animals, and plants need to be strong and healthy.

runoff
Water from farms that flows along the ground until it joins a river or stream.

species
A group of animals or plants that share the same body shape and can breed with one another.

TO LEARN MORE

BOOKS

Gagne, Tammy. *Coral Reef Ecosystems*. Minneapolis: Abdo
Publishing, 2016.

Medina, Nico. *Where Is the Great Barrier Reef?* New York:
Penguin Random House, 2016.

Stefoff, Rebecca. *Corals: Secrets of Their Reef-Making
Colonies*. North Mankato, MN: Capstone Press, 2019.

NOTE TO EDUCATORS

Visit **www.focusreaders.com** to find lesson plans,
activities, links, and other resources related to this title.

INDEX

Answer Key: 1. Answers will vary; **2.** Answers will vary; **3.** B; **4.** C